LATE LOVE
& Other Whodunnits

LATE LOVE
& Other Whodunnits

❧

Diana Hendry

For Chris
with all good
wishes for late love!

Diana Hendry

PETERLOO POETS   MARISCAT PRESS

ISBN 978 0 946588 48 0

Author's Acknowledgements

Thanks are due to the editors of the following magazines and anthologies: *The Herald, The Dark Horse, The London Magazine, Markings, 100 Favourite Scottish Love Poems* (Luath), *Poetry Scotland, The Scotsman, Handfast* (Scottish Poetry Library), *The Hand That Sees* (Scottish Poetry Library), *60/60* (Survivors Press).

    Twelve Lilts: Psalms & Responses was first published by Mariscat Press in 2003. (Translations of *The Psalms in Scots* by Peter Hately Waddell, 1871, coupled with personal responses.) 'Call', 'This is Not a Poem about the River', 'Ten Truths', 'Glenogle Swim Centre, Edinburgh' and 'A Guide Takes Henri Rousseau on a Tour of the Glasshouses of Edinburgh's Royal Botanic Garden' first appeared in *Sparks!* (with Tom Pow) published by Mariscat Press in 2005.

    A version of 'River Boat Stomp' was broadcast on BBC Radio Scotland.

    Acknowledgements are due to the Scottish Arts Council and the National Library of Scotland for the award of a Robert Louis Stevenson Fellowship in 2007, which allowed writing time at Grez-sur-Loing, France — thanks to Fiona Morrison here and Bernadette Plissart there.

    My love and thanks to my poetry-loving kith and kin — my daughter, Kate, Robyn Marsack, Tom Pow, the late William Scammell, Eddie Wainwright, U.A. Fanthorpe and R.V. Bailey.

Cover illustration: 'Once in a Blue Moon', linocut by Willie Rodger, courtesy of the artist and Open Eye Gallery. © Willie Rodger

Designed and typeset by Gerry Cambridge (www.gerrycambridge.com) in Arno Pro, Centaur, Requiem and Typo American Com
Printed by Clydeside Press, 37 High Street Glasgow G1 1LX

Published by Peterloo Poets, The Old Chapel, Sand Lane, Calstock, Cornwall PL18 9QX (www.peterloopoets.com)

and Mariscat Press, 10 Bell Place, Edinburgh EH3 5HT (hamish.whyte@btinternet.com)

Contents

For Hamish II
with love

Reading in Bed

Best bonus of the solitary life,
late hours, the stack beside the bed as good
as a new lover any night. But now
there's all the courtesies to do, of bed-
side lights and sex and sleep and who's the first
to shut up shop. Tonight it's me. Your thrill-
er, *Scorcher*, clearly is. I snuggle in,
conscious that you're close but miles away
(in Florida, to be precise). I lie
and listen as the turn of pages slows
down time. The hush-hush sound your thumb's rub makes
is like the lap of waves that lulls me off,
tucked up in self while you, on night watch, learn
whodunnit, why and when and worlds roll by.

Late Love

At the time, I thought myself
impervious. Bones well padded,
blood running slow, all wildness
knocked right out of me. So when

I first heard them — those low, reedy notes —
I ignored them. I wasn't going to be
disturbed, not now when I was settling
down for cronedom — good deeds maybe,
a little travel, nights in front of the telly.
But then something about the tune

called me. Called with that old quickening
I thought had died in me. Against
my own better judgement, I went
deeper in. And then the shock of him!
Even the dog took fright, shooting
off home, tail between its legs. And
the birds startled up and away
as if they'd never seen the likes.

All I saw was a glimpse
of hairy thighs. A discreet horn,
then that wicked smile. Now
I'm ticklish, itchy, tender, raw,
alert to the moment. Its old sing-song.

Why it took so long

You were otherwise occupied
and so, in a thistledown way, was I.
Also living in the wrong town
and not done with the lunacies of youth
or the worse ones of middle age.
There were children, of course,
taking priority in energy, money, love,
and books to write and much mellowing
and tenderising of the heart to be done
and all the impedimenta of history,
fantasy, expectation to ditch,
and the fire wall to take down,
and the barbed-wire brambles to snip,
and the breast plate to strip,
and the look-out to drug,
and one's mother to silence,
and one's cover to blow,
and one's heart to risk.

Even so, when my waist was slim
and my hair still brown,
where were you?

The Vase

Out of everything in this room that contains
the history of your life before me — the books,
paintings, CDs, endless tacky ornaments
of cats — my eyes light on it. I can't
imagine how its maker has taken the shape
of a bulb and impossibly stretched it
into this delicate, elegant twist of glass
and then, for fun maybe, run a piping
of green icing round its rim, down its sides.

It's lived for so long on this shelf, you take it
for granted. Probably half see it. I begin
to adopt it, sometimes put flowers in it,
buy a small wire brush to try, uselessly,
to ease away the water stains of twenty,
maybe thirty years, woo it with promises
of tlc, daily appreciation. I covet it.

After a year you bring it to me, swaddled
in a towel like a new-born. I try to find
a place where it will look right, feel at home.
Nowhere will do. It's as if I've stolen it.
It's like a step-child taken from home.
No amount of washing and shining,
no sweet-pea posy, no understanding,
can console it. *His*, it says. *His* past.

And hers. Let it alone.

You, going away

can't know all the partings
that echo in this room
as you, in your hat and coat
prepare to leave.

Your train's at eleven forty-five.
I could stay
in the Hall of Departures called home,
wash the plate you ate from,
fold the clothes you left behind
or come to the station.

I wash your plate,
hang up your shirt,
slide heart back inside sleeve,
practise aloneness as a necessary art.

When are you coming back?
The lid of the marmalade jar is stuck.

Application

O let me be your bidie-in
And keep you close within
As dearest kith and kin
I promise I'd be tidy in
Whatever bed or bunk you're in
I'd never ever drink your gin
I'd be your multi-vitamin
I'd wear my sexy tiger-skin
And play my love-sick mandolin
It cannot be a mortal sin
To be in such a dizzy spin
I'd like to get inside your skin
I'd even be your concubine
I hope you know I'm genuine
O let me be your bidie-in.

Punctuation

The Full Stop
Small and deadly —
but put several close together
and who knows what they can lead to ...

The Comma
A sweetie. Polite, unobtrusive,
keeps 'he said' separate
from 'she said' while holding
both together.

The Semi-Colon
Dodgy. Comes over as self-important
while being uncertain of its identity.

The Colon
O catch your breath
for whatever comes next:

The Dash
Exuberant, daring, impetuous, risky —
needs all the others
to keep it steady.
The romantic one.

The Exclamation Mark
All bravado hiding
shyness.

Brackets
(For putting inside
what needs safe-keeping)

Inverted Commas
For words not yet said ...

Against Families

No, I won't go to The Gardens today.
It's a holiday. Families will be rampant.
Right now, at breakfasts all over the city,
mothers are picking crusts off the floor
and children are squirming in their seats
and someone says, *It's a fine day,*
let's go to The Gardens and take a picnic.
And it requires much buttering of bread
and packing of spare macs and hats (in case)
and extra juice for the little one
and fitting the push chair into the boot
and it's all so exhausting it's no wonder
that when they get to the Gardens
they're enveloped in familydom
like the earth in its atmosphere.
                              So that
those of us who are divorced, widowed,
exiled or unreasonably alone, suddenly
suffer a strange invisibility or, at best,
a shifty look from eyes – a multiple
 of eyes – that suggest there is something
 terribly wrong with any individual
walking here alone. A smell perhaps,
or personality disorder. Almost
you can hear their mantra:

We are the family.
We are morality's guardians.
We are the government's darlings.
We are the best idea since polygamy.
We shall inherit the earth —
or at least the Gardens.

Just Blue

Remember that old bottle you dug up from the dump?
It appeared from under a mucky hoard of old
Marmites, Gordons, White Horse Labels.
The sudden blue of it was like the wonder of ocean
after weeks in the city. Milk of Magnesia circa 1906,
its origin and maker's name stamped in raised
glass letters — the *Chas. H. Phillips Chemical Company,
Glenbrook, Connecticut* — we could almost hear
it clinking in the cargo ship in which it came.

Back home you stood at the sink for hours,
wire-brushing out the gunk, thumbing shut
its mouth, making a cocktail shaker
of *Fairy Liquid*, Gloucestershire dump, Atlantic,
until it glowed deep blue. After we split,

sold the house, divided the goods, fixed
custody of the children, I kept the bottle.
Whatever else we lost, this has remained.
It stands on the kitchen shelf, rescued
and washed again. Clean and blue.

Fall-Out

While the war went on, the child
sat in a circle of sunlight. The house shook.
Precarious crockery chattered alarm.
The legs went from under the kitchen table.
Something lay dead on the living-room floor.
The clock flew off. O an heirloom! An heirloom!
Everything spilt. And the dish ran away
with the knife and the ring and the cat's nine lives.

The father howled about the house
blowing the fuses, seizing essentials —
a letter, a photo, his old school tie.
The mother was electrified.
Static frizzled her hair. In a circle
of sunlight the child sat, burning, burning.

About Your New Family

Today, our daughter and yours went shopping in town.
It was a special occasion. Big sister and little sister
who had two pounds forty to spend. I looked after
the dog, kept politely invisible, thought about sisters
and how there's no substitute for a good one.
I pictured them holding hands. Big sister looking back
to herself as little. Little looking forward to herself as big.
This will be their never forgotten adventure.

Ten years and still my bones don't understand
why your daughter isn't also mine. I want to invent
some new, familial title — might-have-been-mum,
mother once removed, mother-in-store.

It being nearly Halloween, your daughter has bought
and lost, glow-in-the-dark fangs, a pair
of front incisors, greenish and costing forty pence.
I'm to buy them again and send them to her.

I could take out my own and send you those.

Big Sister's Coming on a Visit
—for Leila

Clean whole house, polish shoes,
Here's the news —
Big Sister's coming on a visit.

Put on best dress, wait for train,
Pray no rain —
Big Sister's coming on a visit.

Book the taxis, fly the flags,
Hide the fags —
Big Sister's coming on a visit.

Buy up florist, shine the town,
Fetch the crown —
Big Sister's coming on a visit.

Big Sister coming with big big case
Big Sister coming with smiley face
Big Sister coming with big big heart
Big Sister likes playing big big part.

Big Sister coming with little frightened soul
Big Sister nervous as new born foal
Big Sister coming with dodgy knee
Big Sister coming with bravery
Big Sister coming to visit me.

Switch the sun on, banish blues,
Here's the news —
Big Sister's coming on a visit.

Dear Brother in Law and Love
—for George on his birthday

How goes it up on the heights of eighty? I note
Your back's as straight and your legs as long as when
Some sixty years ago my sister brought
You home for inspection. Romantically landed, you kept
Your sailor's eye and need of adventure that took
You off watching whales in the Sea of Cortez; the high
Risk fathering of three blonde daughters; trekking
An ambulance to Herzogivina; up to the top
Of Kilimanjaro. No way can I pack your life
In a sonnet so I'll blur those executive director years
The grit and the grind that left us well-heeled. I think
Of you now in your garden of trees, in the cabin
Of music and books you built for yourself and above
All wish you that whoop of the spirit — the startle of love.

Looking for the Dalai Lama

Of the two or three thousand books in my house,
the only one that might interest my son
is *Transforming the Mind* by the Dalai Lama.
We look for it. Me, my partner, my son,
my son's wife. We spend the two whole days
of my son's visit looking for it.

Paranoic thoughts (that I ought to transform)
suggest any number of friends who might
have nicked it. I lapse into the pagan notion
that my impure motive in wishing to prove
that I am not irredeemably worldly,
has resulted in the book being magicked
away or maybe dissolved into emptiness.
A culture clash prevents me from praying
to St Jude to retrieve it. All we can do

is to carry on searching the shelves
of the sitting room, study, spare room,
kitchen. In the drawers of my desk.
In the bedroom cupboard. My bag.
And every minute it becomes
more urgent as if we are looking
not for a book but each other.

These days my son is so transformed
I hardly recognize him with his shorn head,
latterly dreadlocked, his vegan supper,
whose breakfast was a Mars Bar,
his yogic wife, successor to the blonde
he eloped with to Paris. My son
has grown wise. And distant.

I miss him. We never found the book.

Astanga Poetry
—for my son Hamish I

It is necessary to learn the anatomy
of language, the asanas of speech
until your grammar's so flexible
you can back-bend an image, stand
a simile on its head, sustain
your sutras. Your metaphors may need
adjustment. This can be painful.

A guru is helpful — Pattabi Jois perhaps
or Wm Wordsworth — though you will still
need to find your own way and voice.
Whatever posture/imposture you take up —
warrior, dog, tree, boat, snake — you must
be wholly inside it. About concentration:
this should be light, balanced, alert.
Be humble on your writing pad. Then

there's the breath. The rhythm
of inhalation, exhalation, inspiration,
the tuning in. I've heard the art
compared to the last stage of that
old song and dance, the *hokey cokey*,
when you put your whole self in
then your whole self out. This may
take years of practice. And much sweat.

Milk
—for Kate

I took you off the breast too soon
wanting my self back, my figure, my pen —
yet you came through with such a caul-full of love
I couldn't believe it. Grace-bearer,
spirit like a lit candle,
those pretty feet, those curls,
that passionate temper even then.

Such milk of human kindness, tlc,
daughter-to-mother dearness
you gave to me, you almost starved
yourself to death. No amount
of music, song or words of mine
could make amends.

Honey, here's milk,
full cream, organic, goat's
whatever turns you on.
I'm sending it in crates —
you'll hear the chinking bottles
as the milk float
drifts dreamily, if bumpily,
down your muddy country track.

If I could, I'd send the cow.

To An Unborn Grandchild

I picture you curled up in the dark
Knowing only the pulse of blood,
bump of bone and rib, your mother's
heartbeat. Have you all your toes now?
Are your eyelashes in place?

Get your head down. The head
is always troublesome.
After that it's slither and slide,
blood, mucus, love.

Come easily. Come swiftly.
Come with everything right about you.
Come with a wonderful mix of genes
that takes the best from all of us.

The air will be shocking, I know,
but take a deep breath.
Tell us you've arrived. Cry.

At Miss Foulkes Secretarial College

My father sent me there. Typing, he said
was a skill no girl should be without.
You'll always be able to earn a living.

We all sat Upright
at our Upright Machines and clacked
in Unison. Miss F played music
as we got the rhythm   going.
We were PERCUSSION. Our platens
    whiiiiiiizzzzzzzed
our bells   *trilled,*
we were learning the alphabet
all over again in the grownups' order.
Left hand: **a s d f** – finger across   for **g.**
Right hand: colon **l k j** – finger across   for **h.**
    <u>**do not look down**</u>
at the keys. Soon we will graduate
to words. Soon we will tap tap tap
them out fasterandfaster. Miss F times us with her stop.
Watch.   So many words a minute so many words a minute
somanywords … Nobody told us it was the spaces
             between
that mattered, earning a living, a living,
                 a living in words.

Father's Dogs

All called Sam. In family legend each remembered
for some quirk or foible. Airdale Sam, who'd go halfway round
the block and stop. Boxer Sam, who stole the Sunday roast
from out its pan. And bulldog Sam, a post-war pet,
a Churchill sans cigar. Memento of our finest hour.

Poor ugly mug. Short of breath, long on saliva,
too many hours shut up in the kitchen turned
him nasty. Unwanted when my father died,
he was 'put to sleep' on the funeral pyre,
while that accoutrement, mother's poodle, survived
in triumph. Consumer of chicken. Allowed on the sofa.

Prayer at Sixty

Lord, sixty years and still
My arteries of love run sluggish.
Take thou thy little bottle brush of love
And cleanse my vasculars of mean-minded silt.
Mend thou the pump of generosity
And, while keeping me relatively lean,
Make me big-hearted.

Seven Blessings

For Hamish and Anna on the occasion of their marriage

More to share than to possess
Words that refresh
The forgiving caress
The heart undressed.
Grace to cherish
Friendship to nourish
Love to flourish

Ten Truths

1. Undoubtedly I am a doubtful creature.

2. My eyesight and insight are poor.

3. Testing the statement 'I exist'
   I ask if I'm dreaming.

4. Unless I hallucinated,
   I have two dear children.

5. The sun rose today
   as it did yesterday and the day before.
   I don't take it for granted.

6. Given the choice of truth or mystery,
   I'd choose the latter.

7. Not knowing the truth,
   I wouldn't want you to think I tell lies.

8. Youth is wanting to know.
   Age is glad you don't.

9. Of all things fluid, love is the most.

10. I hope to end on a positive note.
    I'm working towards it. Dredging the dark.

The Songs of Moll

i

And how is Moll today? Fretting
under a canopy of one-liners
and uncomfortable in her skin.
The pimp she works for isn't going
to let her off the hook. Oh no! If
one life isn't large enough for her
then wanting five (or twenty-five)
can only make the one impossible.

Knock a nail in the moment
and shut your eyes, Moll. Peg
your colours etc. The moment
can be larger than five lives.
Consider the pebble in the pool
spreading the moment wide, wide.
Which pebble? Which pebble?
Moll asks. How petulant she is
on a mid morning in Spring.

ii

Well, he said, lolling easy, smiling
his sleazy smile, *have the day off.*
But it was too late for Moll, addicted
as she was to the lyric streets,
hanging about on corners waiting
perhaps for an epic roller. And how
stay in the house with the blinds down
and not a sound from the central heating
boiler or even an occasional sparrow?

iii

Why get evolved with him? Moll's mother asks
from deep down in the underworld. *A nice girl
like you.* And Moll knows she is not
his one and only. Such a soft spot he has
for the American gals — Emily, Elizabeth,
Sylvia. Moll's lucky to catch a few words
out of the side of his mouth, en route
for somewhere, while polishing his toe caps
or smoking a cheroot. *Passing through*
as he says. But lovers can't be choosers.
He has her doing the paper-work,
counting the syllables, how many beats
to the bar and all that. Always promising,
promising to lift the clouds of unknowing.
Oh yea? But Moll's a push-over when
it comes to a few sweet nothings.

iv

In the resounding silence
Moll hears the world twirl.
Nine hundred and ninety nine kilometres an hour
in London. So many delusions, stillness
being the first. It's enough to make
Moll dizzy and rain all day yesterday.
Moll is very damp of spirits, ditto
suede jacket, spotted all over shoulders
due to under-small umbrella. Also guilty
considering slaughter of lamb, mole, rabbit,
deer, whatever. Maybe died of natural.
Who are you kidding, Moll? The why,
when and how of her own natural or
unnatural keep Moll in a spin all night.

v

Apart from the pimp, there is She of the Order
of dust, polish, mop who inhabits Moll's house
forever straightening things out, a fanatic
for putting away wherof, thinks Moll,
there are many childish things, not to mention
Aunt B put away for the careless loss of soul
one dark night, whither whither no-one knows
and the many memos in Moll's skull
all irretrievably put away each in a little cell
of its ownio so far back as is the box under
the bed of secrets white yellow and blue.
Some days Moll considers putting away
She of the Order, maybe in a cupboard
locked or along with Aunt B, that forgotten
night with Luigi or the story in the blue box.

vi

Moll's favourite song — *Little Dolly Daydreams*
which she sings in the ambulance on the way
to the funny farm in Wild Country Lane where
Molls puts on the poet's brown leather jacket,
becomes Cleopatra, is carried off in a male nurse's arms
to her very own cell. Is it when the world
makes sense and everything — like the miracle
of water gushing from a tap — speaks in symbols
that the serious man in a suit says *you are very ill*?
How Moll laughs on this Good/Bad Friday.

Psalm 12

David's lament for the dearth of honest folk;
but the Lord will save his own from lies and jeering.

Save us, Lord, for the good man's gone
and loyal folk dwindle. Falsehoods are cracked,
neighbour to neighbour, all's gush and gas
and double-dealing; all's brag and gab.

The Lord shall lop the flatterer's lip,
the gossip's uncouth tongue, those
who boast, *We'll master the masses*
with blah and blether. Who can lord it
over us? We'll say what we like.

For the grief of the weak, for the sighs of the poor,
now must I rise up, says the Lord,
and keep them safe from those who jeer.
The words of the Lord are pure as silver
seven times proven in a kiln of clay.

Guard us, Lord, from this generation.
When the dregs rise to the top,
hypocrites flourish on every side.

P.S to Psalm 12

'... with flattering lips and with a double heart do they speak.'

From sex-pots and spin-docs and celebrity sweeties
and ads that sell wrinkle-free age

Good Lord, deliver us!

Psalm 23

The sheep-keeping of the Lord is kind
and canny with a brave home at the last;
David keeps his sheep, the Lord keeps David

The Lord's my shepherd, no want shall befall me.
He allows me to lie among soft growing grasses,
He leads me along the wind-quietened waters.

He wakens my woeful soul with whispers of wisdom
And sets me on the right road.

If now I should go through the dead mirk-dale
I'll dread no scaithing for Yourself are near-by me
Your stick and your staff, they keep me most cheery.
My food You've provided in the face of my foes.
On my head You have drizzled the sweetness of oil.
My beaker is full to overflowing.
Now shall goodness and guidance go with me
All the days of my life. And evermore
In the Lord's own house, at long last, I shall bide.

Shepherds

I saw a shepherd on the Isle of Skye
who rode a motor-bike, his collie straddled
across his knees. Another, hospiced
in Dumfries, told how he dipped
and tagged the sheep to save them from ticks,
helped with the difficult birth of a lamb,
defended the new-born against the crows.

But David's man? We could do with him here,
out searching the mirk-dales of the mind,
providing the dip that cools the endless nag
of wants, defending the old against
the greedy cancer crows. Work enough
to round us up, each in the hubris of
an individual fleece, acting tough,
though lost, silly, and never loved enough.

Psalm 102

(lines 1 – 11)

A prayer for the feckless when feeling forsaken
he tips out his troubles before the Lord

Lord, let this prayer win its way to you.
Reach down and speak home to me
Here, where my days reek of smoke
Where my hearth-stone's blackened
Where such dread swells through me
My heart's burnt to stubble.
I'm worn to the bone with grief
And keening, am like the curlew
That calls in the wasteland, the owl
In the desert, the sparrow who watches
Alone from the roof top. Day after day
Ill-willers jeer and rant madly against me.
Faced by the rough of Your fury
My breakfast's ashes, my soup is tears,
For You have hoisted me up, dangled
Me down and thrown me aside
So that my days dwindle to shadows
And I wither like grass.

Late Call

Lord, this is pip-squeak calling.
Even with your infinite technology
I expect your line's busy. Therefore
forgive me my witter, tucked up
as I am in my comfy-comfy
with the telly and all its disasters on.
I expect you've seen. I expect
eternity's in Widescreen.

I hardly like to mention my imaginary
ills, the disturbance in my head,
the way I can't live with you or without.
I run out of usefulness. Grow fat
with anxiety. On a fine morning
I rejoice in your mystery. At night
I listen to your silence and despair.
Dread whatever end's in store.

Attend , Lord, those in valid agony.
I'm just one of the whingers —
though perhaps, as an aside,
you could help me to age as beech leaves do,
transparent enough to let sunshine through.

Psalm 138

A song of praise to the Lord, who's good.

I shall sing to You, Lord, with my whole heart.
I shall sing to You, Lord, before all gods.
I shall kneel to You, Lord, in Your holy house.
I shall sing of Your name, of Your pity and truth,
of the promise You made that higher than all
shall be Your name and Your word.

On the day when I cried out, You heard
and doubled the strength of my soul.
All the kings of the land would praise You, Lord,
if they could but hear You speak.
Loudly they'd lilt the ways of the Lord,
the long-sighted Lord whose scan is vast.
From His great height He respects the humble.
The proud He keeps at a distance.

Though I struggle along, You hold my life sound.
Against the wrath of my rivals You raise one hand
while in the other You hold me safe.

The Lord shall do all this for me.
Your goodness endures for ever, Lord.
Such as I am, I'm the work of your hand.
Surely You'd not altogether fling it by.

A Low Lilt

He likes my song, said the Wind,
My whoosh and whisper, my fugal voices.

He likes my song, said the Sea,
My rush and roar, my orchestration.

He likes my song, said the Rain,
My drip and drum, my timpani.

He likes my song, said the Light,
My shadow dance, my flamenco and shimmy.

He likes my song, said the Dark,
For I beat time.

My song isn't ready, said the Man,
I must keep trying.

Psalm 150

The final Hallelujah, very high and grand,
made with all that can dirl and blow.

Hallelujah! Give praise to God in His holy place,
Give Him praise in the stronghold of heaven.
Praise all His wonders and the might of His makings,

With the toot of the horn, with the lute and the harp,
With the drum and the drone and the dance, give Him praise!
With the strings' delight, with the cymbals' dash,
With the cymbals dirling high, praise Him!

With every breath you take, praise Him.

The Drummer

Though he says he doesn't believe,
when he beats the big drum
and when he sets the high-hat dirling
and the crash cymbal crashing
and the splash cymbal splashing
and the riveted cymbal with the shimmering rattle, rattling
and the finger cymbals chinging
and the clackers clacking
and the tom-toms tomming
and the snare drum snaring —
then a certain trance-like look
comes over his sideways face
as though he's listening in
to that heart-beat rhythm
which we all begin with or
maybe tuning in
to earth's hidden pulse,
either way, he's in time and out
and might well be reaching
a hallelujah experience
or something very like,
like happiness.

Last Post

i.m. William Scammell

Bitter bright autumn's come
and nights are drawing sadness in
while you talk of *the final test*
and Henry James greeting death
with *Ah, the distinguished thing.*

Here's an indignant note
to say you can't go off like this
who've been my constant and my kin
through thick and thin affairs of heart
and pen. How should I bear

the years without the tie-beam
of your light on late into
the watches of the night? No-one
talks books like you or can bat a lyric
high above the nets

of time with one swift serve.
I see the Muses of the Lakes
gather like angels at your gate.
They drift across your van Gogh field
and send, as harbinger,

one small black cat who's come
to keep you company in these
hard times. Dear Bill, false comfort's not
the pill for you. When all's made clear
it's love that most distinguishes us —

and cradles you.

To W.S. Graham

Here I am talking to you across
all those years ago or none,
catching your voice on the sound
waves or maybe the sea waves.

Ridiculous man! What a way
to live — cadging money, squandering
yourself on drink, scribbling, scribbling,
talking to ghosts in the night. *I am,*
you wrote, *a nervous man, feeling
unloved and greedy and lyrically manic.*
'O come to my arms my beamish boy'.

Back then, in time was now, when
you read your poems in a Scots parlando,
you towed my heart out beyond the safe reaches.

I would like to find some good words
for you. Ones that you'd like
that are not too fancy. Ones
that would help me come clear.

Sidney, there's such a hullabaloo
of poet voices out there that
it's hard to hear oneself speak.
But now here you are again, new
and newly *Collected*, interrupting
the silence with your wild tap tapping,
trying to speak — as you always did —
from one aloneness to another

or all of us alone together.

Big Man
i.m. Philip Toynbee

There was the day he rode up in biking leathers
having just read *Zen and the Art of*; and the time
he turned his home into a commune, then found
he couldn't live in it; and the water garden he made
with falls and fountains that tumbled enthusiasm.
Soon after, the drop into depression and ECT
described as 'a kind of prayer'. He was one

of those whose body and soul was too big
for comfort, who spent his life seeking
the best way to live, who towards the end
thought himself 'so thick-skinned, so earthy'
that it was 'an impossible task' for God to reach him.

Another mistake.

The Visit

They came with their grief,
brought it into our house —
the great excess baggage of it.
It was beyond our ken,
beyond our wanting to know.

The tragic details of death —
the coroner's inquest, the clearing
up of a life, the funeral arrangements —
we could cope with, offering
tea, whisky, listening.

But this massive, unconsolable grief,
invisible, intangible but as all pervasive
as if their dead boy was everywhere with them —
even feeling the edges of that
cut us to the quick — with our own sons out there
now vulnerably, unfairly alive.

The Man with Three Legs

From the Department of Orthopaedic Surgery,
University of St. Andrews

'In the autumn of 1948 a message was received from a rural practioner stating that in the course of a vist he had discovered a man who, from the cursory glance that had been permitted, had a large sacral appendage with the appearance of a massive tail.'

The Mother

He was a monster, yes,
but he was my monster and I loved him.
His father would have done away with him
when he saw that limb, that leg
with its curled up foot hung from behind
like a huge tail. Always between prayer
and drink, my man. Said he'd been sent
as a punishment for our sins — *your sins*
he'd say, looking at me mad-eyed
for he'd rather the boy was not his at all.
The runt of the litter, he'd say, *that freak.*

His brothers and sisters were sworn
to secrecy with the threat of the belt or worse.
I'd take him out in the pram. Until he was ten
I could hide him in that. We'd walk in the woods.
I'd sing to him. He'd sing back.
I hoped the thing would fall off or shrivel away.
I dreamt I'd wake one morning and find it
on the floor and him as normal as the others.
When he was too big for the pram
I bought him a kilt. And when he grew out
of the kilt I made him a long flannel gown.
O the shame of him. And the blessing.

My youngest who I loved the most
and kept most hidden.

A Local

As bairns we cried him Frankenstein —
Frankie fir short. He was oor monster,
ken whit ah mean? Fowk said how
he'd be oot at gloamin in the woods
happed in a lang sark, nae breeks
an wi this awfy tail hingin oot ahint him.

Maw telt me no tae be daft. She said
he's naebit a puir body who mendit watches.
We didnae believe her. We thocht him a deil,
hauf mannie, hauf beastie. Me an ma pals
wid daur each ither tae throw clabber and chuckies. We'd shout
and laugh tae see him fleein hame.

From the Department of Orthopaedic Surgery,
University of St. Andrews

'The operation consisted of little more than careful dissection through
fibro-fatty tissue. Any difficulty lay in the pre-op preparation of the skin
and then in fashioning suitable skin flaps. We thought we'd gained his
confidence during the unsavoury task of preparing his skin and suggested he celebrate his successful treatment with a shave and a haircut. The
suggestion was received in silence and disregarded. He showed neither
pleasure nor gratitude. The post-operative photograph was secured at
the second attempt only after angry words and our accusation of ungra-
cious behaviour.'

The Patient

Those photographs! Essential
for the treatment plan, they said.
Me, stood there bollock naked before
strangers! Even with my back to them,
even in the polite medical silence,
I heard the ghost of my father
calling me *freak*. I could tell
they were writing their paper
in their heads. I ask you,
who can photograph the mind or the heart?

They expected to be thanked
for making me 'normal'.
Suggested 'a change of personality'.
Gave me trousers. All I felt
was loss, as if what had been
taken away was who I was —
father's freak, mother's blessing.

Afterwards, I stayed home, mending watches,
seeing no-one. A stranger to myself.

From the Department of Orthopaedic Surgery,
University of St. Andrews. Postscript

'In spite of our hopes to the contrary, it became evident that this unfortunate
man had lived too long with this tumour to change his ways. He returned to his
room and his watches and was not seen outside the house. Whatever plans he
had for the future, his new-found freedom proved short lived. He died unex-
pectedly at his home three months later from an acute infection of the urinary
tract.'

Museum visitor

In its glass box, the leg
looks like a joint of meat.
I can picture it in the oven.
It would feed about ten.

The exhibit is entitled
Supplementary Appendage. Leg.

River Boat Stomp, New Orleans

Despite the order to abandon your pets,
No way was he going to leave his dogs behind.
They were winching people out by helicopter.
In the stadium thousands of folk
Were desperate to bus out of town.
Dead bodies floated in his street.
Drinking water was running out. But no-one,
No-one was going to shift him
Out of this place without his dogs. No, sir!

They must have cursed
Such bloody-minded stubborness
And the dogs wouldn't thank him
As they hoisted all seven
Into a flat-bottomed skiff
To take the Lord knows where.

And you could call him crazy or selfish —
There being so many human lives to save —
Or think that he was just one of those men
Who find dogs easier to love than people.
But then you have to ask yourself

Does the *kind* of love matter?
Does what you'd risk your life for matter?
Or only that you've love enough to risk it?

Black Dog

Here he comes, padding
across the surface of your mind
at the first sniff of sadness.
He weighs a ton. Looks at you
with those post-Hiroshima eyes
until the silent howl of him sinks deep
into your gut. What does he want?

You feed him all the hurts you've got.
He can't get enough of it, love, love.
He wants his mammy. He wants
to be back in the womb with his paws
over his eyes. He wants. He wants.

Poor black dog with the wildness
trapped in him and nowhere to go.
Toss him your funny bone,
let him gnaw on that.

A Guide takes Henri Rousseau on a Tour of the Glasshouses of Edinburgh's Royal Botanic Garden

Colours? You want bright colours?
Let me show you the Glory Bush. Its flowers
remind me of purple satin. Perhaps you'd prefer
the scarlet Bugler from Java or the coral pink
of the passion flower? Here's everyone's favourite —
the bottle-brush plant, such a jolly ochre. And just look
at the Jade Vine! Peppermint green I'd call that.
See how it dangles its claw-like flowers?

Tigers have claws too? Indeed, sir. Let's move on
to the Palm House. *You think you've seen one?*
Eating an antelope? Well it is dark and steamy.
We have curly palms, kentia palms, cabbage palms
and this one trying to escape through the ceiling,
is *Sabal bermudana*, the Indian fan, at least
two hundred years old. *Now the antelope's crying?*
Well it's not surprising. Oh! Spot the bananas!
Monkeys? Eating oranges? No, sir. Not in our plan.

You like the exotic? Well, let's say hello
to the Amazonian lily, the sacred lotus,
and these huge, wild ancestors of the African violet.

You can see a dark woman playing a flute?
And snakes sliding out of the trees? One's draped
round her neck? Best to stay calm, sir.
The lady's often here at dusk — fond of the Garden
I'm told and quite a charmer. Let's slip out quietly.

This Is Not A Poem About The River

About the black zip on the heron's throat
And the mantra he uttered all on one note,
Not a word I'll let slip.

The shifty willows' hushed palaver,
The weir unrolling its roll of silver,
My blind eye shall skip.

On the vows of the lovers who met by chance,
And the cause of the midges' frantic dance
I'll never unzip.

The sun panning gold in dazzled distraction,
The moon mooning over its broken reflection,
In my pocket I'll keep.

Light dipping its brush in Turner's pots
And night smudging shadows to inky blots
I'll send soundless to sleep.

About the angst of the frog, the dream of the trout
And the stories jiggled and tossed about
No poem shall plop.

To the driftwood of myth, the rapids of time,
The maestro of rhythm, the babbbler of rhyme
I'll add the full stop.

The heart of darkness, the water of life,
The source of meaning, the sea's fluent wife,
I'll bottle and sip.

The gulls' raw answer to Charon's news
I'll never pass on to the greedy muse.

Into silence I'll slip.

Glenogle Swim Centre, Edinburgh

Up and down up and down up and down I go (**one**) called here
as by a mullah calling me to Health at ungodly hour (**two**) of
eight a.m. breaststroking up backstroking down possessed of
idée fixe twenty lengths much as the Lord has three (**three**)
score years and ten in His or so it's said and is He in the swim
no He is not He is above it all (**four**) upping and downing as
repeat of breakfast dinner tea and much (**five**) as tomorrow and
tomorrow and tomorrow (**six**) creeps on a petty pace though
creeping is not what I (**seven**) do sometimes the crawl pretend-
ing to be fish arm over ear over arm over ear flip flap of fish-tail
feet could be fins (**eight**) nice to have gills monotony they say
can give (**nine**) way to revelation through my goggles I see by
glimpses (**ten**) now goggled in Glenogle and ear-plugged too
such sensory deprivation and O how I love them (**eleven**) the
others distracting me from the tee-hee-hee-dium of the self
self self (**twelve**) those swimming in lanes the narrow traps of
straight and (**thirteen**) narrow moral horror the old men gossip-
ing (**fast one fourteen**) in the shallows and she who gets on my
wick always hogging (**fifteen**) the inside lane in never-get-hair
wet cap (**sixteen**) even the the ladies known as *the minesweepers*
for swimming three abreast chatty happy as they go and (**sev-
enteen**) turning my up and downing into round (**eighteen**)
abouting and Jimmy singing *Come Fly With Me* who is maybe
seeking another element though this (**nineteen**) if there were
sky above and infinity before and behind and if it were only sea
spread vast and deep is mine so sometimes you (**twenty**) have
to make do and of course I enjoy it.

Visionary

Praise be the one who with no other technical assistance
than a ladder, bucket and soapy sponge allows me to see
the garden, my neighbours, the sky newly washed
and all without the aid of lenses or laser.
Who with a few strokes of his scraper debunks January's weather.
Who entertains me with his acrobatic skill —
one foot on an outside window sill, the other in —
for which, hopefully he is covered by his insurance, not mine.
Who lustrates my fanlight, dormer, sash and bay with his baptismal
lathering
and baby bubbles. Who keeps his equipment
in the pocket of a sexy apron hung around his hips.
Who doesn't drip. Who asks only for ten quid and tea with two
sugars.
Who telescopes his ladder with a cheery clank-clunk.
Who empties his bucket down an outside drain.
Who has no idea I'm about to write him an ode in praise.
Who departs leaving me a glimpse of infinity that lasts
with luck, a full five mintues before the rain.

The death of head-waiters

The place brought back memories
of Fifties hotels — the five star ones
in south coast resorts like Bognor
or Bexhill — with windows that glistened
over promenade and polished sea
and a head-waiter who led you to your table
with a strut that said he was far grander
than you. And maybe a show on the pier
after dinner, or a subdued sink into chintz,
a nod at a sea-view, a discreet drink.

This one — with its empty whisky bar,
its revolving door that no longer revolves,
its ancient décor and packeted breakfast,
its bath which runs with harbour mud,
its smell of stale grandeur,
its comfortably sad decline, its suggestion
that all head-waiters have died —
never had that many stars
and those it had are waning fast.

I stand on the porterless porch,
face the bracing sea
and feel immeasurably glad
the past has passed for me.

The Gas Man Cometh

at seven twenty-five a.m.
with his hoover, a little brush and a blackening spray
for the unreal coals of my 'real flame' fire.

He cometh without dust-sheets
and lolleth on my rug
and telleth me at length about his gout
and what the doctor said
and how his mate died just last year
and only fifty-one
and he taketh all of ten minutes
and he chargeth me thirty-five quid
and leaveth me blazing.

The Cowboy Experience
—for Susie Maguire

It was a present. My fiftieth birthday.
You go, she says. *You must have watched*
every Western ever made. Go live it, my love.
I'll stay home and watch the 450 episodes
of East Enders that I've missed.

So I packed my stetson, boots and spurs, slung
my holster round my hips — my hips aren't bad,
though I say it myself — and off I went. Out West.

When I arrived there was a Wells Fargo stagecoach
waiting for me and this guy who tipped his hat
and drawled *Howdy Pardner*. Then off we rolled,
over the prairie. Out West. So naturally

when the Indians appeared, I thought they were part
of the package. Even admired their bows and arrows,
they looked so convincing. *Gee pardner*, I said —
I was catching the lingo — *Ain't that something!*
Ain't that swell! Then the arrow twanged past
my head and another came after and then blood
was staining my pants and my pardner was a dot
galloping hellforleather into the sunset.

Thank god for the movies. I knew
what I had to do. I bit the dust.

Call

All our angels are busy right now
Your call has been placed in a queue.

We are the queue
We are the patient ones
Waiting for angels
to unbusy themselves
and answer our call.
'Speak to us.
Why do you never speak? Speak.'

My room is narrow.
The velux window shows a screen-saver of clouds.
My hand is clammy on the phone, listening
for the phantom listeners of the queue.

Thank you for your patience.
Please continue to hold.

We are the queue
We are the patient ones
Waiting for angels
'Living and partly living'
Alone and not alone.

The clouds have changed to giddy stars
receding in the dark of outer space
and I am falling aeons into emptiness,
foetal-curled and tumbling from the tower.

Where are the firemen
with their catching blanket?
Where is the angel
with the rope of kindness?

Your call is important to us.
All our angels are busy. Please
continue to hold.

Free-falling in wide-open space
I hear the listeners' conch-shell whispers
calling as at school's morning registration,
'Here!' 'Here!' 'Here!' 'Here!'

Harbours
—for U.A. Fanthorpe and R.V. Bailey

Not that I believe in them
despite all those symbolic *Roget* suggestions —
refuge, place of safety, making it to port.

But just set me down anywhere near one
and I'm all boat, furled sails, an outboard motor
in my throat, oil in lieu of blood, nets
instead of veins, oilskins for flesh

and either I can snug up against the harbour wall,
(leaving the sheets to clink musically against the mast)
and climb the iron ladder to where my dog
is barking and dancing a welcome or
I can unwind the rope from its stud, fix my eye
on the narrow opening out to everywhere
and slowly set forth. It's early morning of course,
before the world's awake. You'll hear the phut-phut,
a sea churn, my boots in the cabin.

I want you to know this is an English harbour
born out of Masefield and ferries and the tug
to leave and the pull to come home.